Labrador Retrievers

Kelley MacAulay & Bobbie Kalman

Photographs by Marc Crabtree

🌳 Crabtree Publishing Company

www.crabtreebooks.com

Labrador Retrievers
A Bobbie Kalman Book

Dedicated by Margaret Amy Salter
To Gene Prall, who is on a magical adventure with his lab, Casey.

Editor-in-Chief
Bobbie Kalman

Writing team
Kelley MacAulay
Bobbie Kalman

Substantive editor
Kathryn Smithyman

Editors
Molly Aloian
Michael Hodge
Robin Johnson
Rebecca Sjonger

Design
Katherine Kantor

Production coordinator
Heather Fitzpatrick

Photo research
Crystal Foxton

Consultant
Dr. Michael A. Dutton, DVM, DABVP, Weare Animal Hospital,
www.weareanimalhospital.com

Special thanks to
Alexander Makubuya, Lakme Mehta-Jones, Owen Mehta-Jones,
Shilpa Mehta-Jones, Samara Parent, Bailee Setikas, Shelbi Setikas,
Sheri Setikas, Katrina Sikkens, Judy Lewandowski and Buckley,
Cindy Parson and Lily, Julie Plata and Jake

Photographs
All photos by Marc Crabtree except:
© Lisa Roy. Image from BigStockPhoto.com: page 26
Bruce Coleman Inc.: Gail M. Shumway: page 27
Phanie/Photo Researchers, Inc.: page 7
Comstock: page 18 (milk, meat, and egg)
Ingram Photo Objects: page 18 (chocolate)
Photodisc: pages 4, 18 (top)

Illustrations
Margaret Amy Salter: page 18

Library and Archives Canada Cataloguing in Publication

MacAulay, Kelley
    Labrador retrievers / Kelley MacAulay & Bobbie Kalman.

(Pet care)
Includes index.
ISBN-13: 978-0-7787-1762-1 (bound)
ISBN-10: 0-7787-1762-3 (bound)
ISBN-13: 978-0-7787-1794-2 (pbk.)
ISBN-10: 0-7787-1794-1 (pbk.)
    1. Labrador retriever--Juvenile literature. I. Kalman, Bobbie, date.
II. Title. III. Series: Pet care

SF429.L3M33 2006   j636.752'7   C2006-904091-5

Library of Congress Cataloging-in-Publication Data

MacAulay, Kelley.
  Labrador retrievers / Kelley MacAulay & Bobbie Kalman ;
photographs by Marc Crabtree.
    p. cm. -- (Pet care)
Includes index.
  ISBN-13: 978-0-7787-1762-1 (rlb)
  ISBN-10: 0-7787-1762-3 (rlb)
  ISBN-13: 978-0-7787-1794-2 (pbk)
  ISBN-10: 0-7787-1794-1 (pbk)
    1. Labrador retriever--Juvenile literature. I. Kalman, Bobbie. II. Title.
III. Series.

SF429.L3M33 2006
636.752'7--dc22
    2006018064

Crabtree Publishing Company

www.crabtreebooks.com   1-800-387-7650

Published in Canada
Crabtree Publishing
616 Welland Ave.
St. Catharines, ON
L2M 5V6

Published in the United States
Crabtree Publishing
PMB16A
350 Fifth Ave., Suite 3308
New York, NY 10118

Published in the United Kingdom
Crabtree Publishing
White Cross Mills
High Town, Lancaster
LA1 4XS

Published in Australia
Crabtree Publishing
386 Mt. Alexander Rd.
Ascot Vale (Melbourne)
VIC 3032

Contents

What are labrador retrievers?

Labrador retrievers, or "labs," are a kind of dog. Dogs are **mammals**. Mammals are animals that have **backbones**. A backbone is a row of bones in the middle of an animal's back. Mammals have hair or fur on their bodies. A baby mammal drinks milk from its mother's body.

A lab's body

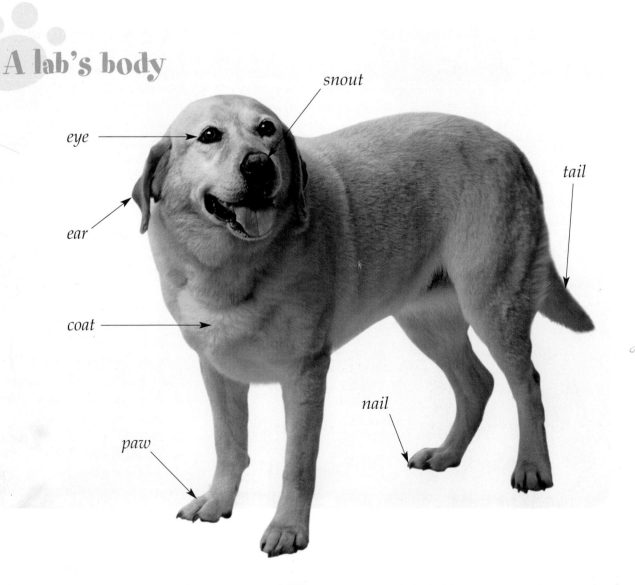

snout

eye

tail

ear

coat

nail

paw

Lovely labs

Labs are big, strong dogs. They grow to be 21 to 25 inches (53-64 cm) tall. Most labs weigh between 55 and 75 pounds (25-34 kg). Male labs can weigh over 100 pounds (45 kg), however! Labs have coats that are black, yellow, or **chocolate**. Chocolate labs are brown.

*Some people think that the color of a lab's coat **affects** its personality. For example, they think black labs are more protective than yellow or chocolate labs are. That is not true! The color of a lab's coat does not affect its personality.*

Working dogs

Labs first came from Newfoundland, Canada. Hundreds of years ago, labs were popular with Newfoundland **fishers**. Labs helped fishers pull in heavy nets full of fish from rivers and streams. Labs also ran into water to **retrieve**, or bring in, fish that escaped from the nets. Many hunters also used labs. After the hunters shot birds, the labs ran to retrieve them.

People like working with labs because most labs are friendly dogs. Labs are also popular pets because they are so friendly.

Still working

Today, many labs have important jobs. More than half of all **guide dogs** in North America are labs. Guide dogs are specially **trained** to help people who are **physically challenged**. Many labs are also **therapy dogs**. People bring therapy dogs to hospitals to cheer up patients.

Volunteers raise and train guide dogs. Once the dogs are trained, they go to live with people who are physically challenged.

Super sniffers

Some labs are trained to help people during **emergencies**. For example, labs can often help locate people who are buried in **avalanches**. The dogs are able to sniff out people who are buried beneath the snow.

The right pet for you?

Labs make wonderful pets. They are loyal, gentle, and fun to play with. Caring for a lab is not easy, however. Labs need a lot of attention. They do not like to be alone. They also have a lot of energy! Your lab will need plenty of exercise every day. You will have to spend time training your lab, as well.

Keeping your lab happy and healthy will take a lot of work.

Are you ready?

Before you decide to get a lab, gather your family together and answer the questions below.

- Labs need room to run around. Do you have enough space for a lab?

- Who will feed your lab every day?

- Labs like to be with people. Will someone be home with your lab throughout the day?

- Labs need healthy food and a lot of toys. Is your family prepared to pay to feed, to care for, and to entertain a lab?

- Labs need to be **groomed**, or brushed and cleaned. Are you willing to keep your lab clean?

- Labs shed a lot of fur! Will you clean up after your lab every day?

Labs live for ten to thirteen years. Are you willing to care for your lab for many years?

The perfect lab

Before you buy a lab, ask your friends and **veterinarian**, or "vet," if they know of any labs that are being given away. You can check **animal shelters** in your area to see if they have any labs. You can also get a lab from a **breeder** or a pet store. Make sure you get a lab from people who take good care of animals!

Proof in the papers

If you want proof that your lab is **purebred**, get your pet from a breeder. A purebred dog has parents and grandparents of the same **breed**, or kind. The breeder should be able to give you papers that prove your lab's parents and grandparents are also labs.

Choosing your lab

Make sure you pick a lab that is healthy and seems to like you. The lab you choose should have:

- a lot of energy
- clean teeth
- clear, shiny eyes
- clean ears with no wax inside
- a clean snout, bottom, and coat
- no sores on its skin
- a smooth, shiny coat with no bald patches

Spend time with a lab before choosing it as your pet.

Little labs

When choosing your lab, you will have to decide whether to get an adult dog or a **puppy**. A puppy is a baby dog. Puppies are cute and a lot of fun. They love to play. Puppies are harder to care for than adult dogs are, however.

It is easy to become attached to a puppy. Remember that you still need to love the puppy when it grows up, however. Adult labs are also cute and fun!

Puppy needs

A puppy needs people around it all the time. A puppy may bark a lot at night or chew things in your house. It needs to be fed many times a day. If you and your family do not have a lot of time to care for a puppy, you may want to get an older lab.

12

Housebreaking

If you choose an older lab, it may be **housebroken** already. Dogs that are housebroken know to go to the bathroom outdoors. If you get a puppy, you will have to housebreak it. About ten minutes after your puppy eats or drinks, put it on its leash and take it outdoors. Take your puppy to the same spot each time. Praise your puppy when it goes to the bathroom outdoors. If you are **consistent** in the training, your puppy will learn to get your attention when it needs to go outdoors.

Be patient while you are housebreaking your lab. Spread papers around your home to protect the floors while your lab is learning.

Preparing for your lab

You will need certain supplies to care for your lab properly. Make sure you have all the supplies before you bring your lab home.

Your lab will need a water bowl and a food bowl.

Buy some treats for your dog. You can use the treats as rewards when you train your lab.

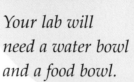

collar

tag

*Your pet should always wear a **collar** and a **tag** with your phone number on it. You can also have your dog **microchipped**. If your pet gets lost, people can use the tag or microchip to return your pet to you.*

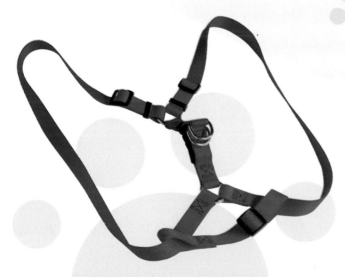

*A big dog like a lab is easier to walk if it is wearing a **harness**. The harness wraps around the front of your lab's body.*

Attach a leash to the harness to keep your lab from running away.

Your lab should have its own bed for sleeping.

Your lab will enjoy having a large **crate** to use as a **den**, or a safe space.

Brush your lab's coat with a **bristle brush**.

Your lab will need its own toothbrush.

Get some dog **nail clippers** to trim your lab's nails.

Labs love to play with toys! Your lab will enjoy having toys to chew on and balls and Frisbees to chase.

Room to roam

Labs need a lot of space. They like to run around and play—both indoors and outdoors! The best home for a lab is a country home with a lot of fenced-in land. A lab will also be happy in a house that has a fenced-in yard. A lab that lives in an apartment will need to get a lot of exercise every day.

Labs have very strong tails that can easily knock things off tables and low shelves. Do you have enough space in your home for a lab?

Run, run, run!

A short walk around the block will not be enough exercise for your lab. Labs need to run! Allowing your dog time outdoors to run around every day is not a treat—it is a requirement. Labs gain weight easily. If your lab does not get enough exercise, it will soon become overweight. Overweight labs are not as healthy as fit labs are. Running around will also help keep your lab happy!

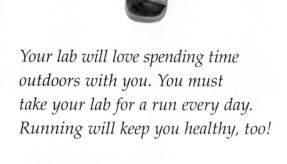

Your lab will love spending time outdoors with you. You must take your lab for a run every day. Running will keep you healthy, too!

Food for labs

Labs love to eat! Ask your vet which dog food to give your lab. A lab needs to eat a complete, balanced dog food that is right for the dog's lifestyle. For example, a young, active lab should eat a dog food made for active dogs.

Your lab always needs a bowl of fresh drinking water. Change the water each day.

Dangerous foods

Certain foods are not safe for your lab to eat. Some foods that are unsafe for your lab are listed below.

- Never give your lab a bone to chew on. Your lab could choke on it.

- It is not safe for dogs to eat even small amounts of chocolate.

- **Dairy foods**, raw meat, and raw eggs can all make your lab sick!

Two feedings

Labs eat their food quickly. When labs eat too fast, their stomachs **bloat**, or swell up. A lab can become very sick if its stomach bloats too much. Feed your lab two meals every day. With two feedings, your pet will not get too hungry, and it will eat more slowly.

Hungry puppies

A lab puppy needs three feedings a day until it is five months old. To feed your puppy, add some hot water to **kibble**, or dry dog food, to make the food softer. Let the food cool. Then add some canned dog food. When your puppy is six months old, begin feeding it twice a day.

Feed adult dog kibble to your lab puppy. Kibble made for puppies has a lot of fat that can cause labs to gain too much weight.

Important training

A lab's energy and strength can cause it to be destructive in your home. Spend fifteen to twenty minutes each day training your lab to behave. Most labs are good at following **commands**, or instructions. Be patient while your lab learns.

Stay!

You should train your lab to "stay." Use treats to help your lab learn. Show your pet a treat. Press gently on your pet's bottom until it sits down. Look into your lab's eyes and say "stay." Hold out your hand flat in front of you with your palm facing the lab as you say "stay." Take a few steps back. After a minute, call your lab to you and give it the treat and a lot of praise!

Learning takes time

As you train your lab, remember that your pet wants to please you. Praise your lab every time it behaves. If your lab is not behaving, be patient. Never hit or yell at your dog. These actions will make your lab afraid of you.

Spend time playing with your lab after training each day. It will soon look forward to its training.

Play time!

Labs love to chase and chew on things. Make sure your lab has about five toys with which it can play. If you give your lab more toys than this, it will treat everything around it as a toy! Put some other dog toys away in a cupboard. Switch your pet's toys about once a month to keep the toys interesting.

Toys made of rubber are safe for your lab to chew on. You can put some food into a hollow rubber chew toy. Your lab will keep busy trying to get the treat!

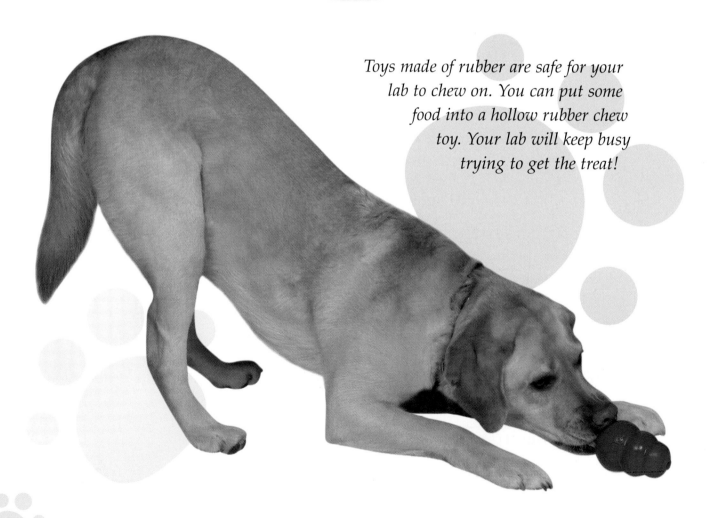

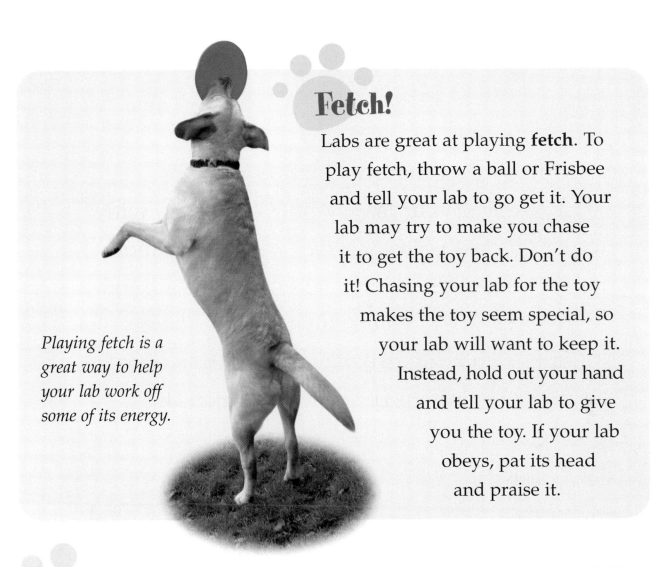

Fetch!

Labs are great at playing **fetch**. To play fetch, throw a ball or Frisbee and tell your lab to go get it. Your lab may try to make you chase it to get the toy back. Don't do it! Chasing your lab for the toy makes the toy seem special, so your lab will want to keep it. Instead, hold out your hand and tell your lab to give you the toy. If your lab obeys, pat its head and praise it.

Playing fetch is a great way to help your lab work off some of its energy.

Hide-and-seek

Your lab will also enjoy playing hide-and-seek with you! Have a friend gently hold on to your lab while you hide inside your home. Then call out to your lab. It will have fun trying to find you!

When your pet finds you, reward it with a treat!

Super swimmers

Swimming is a fun way for your lab to get exercise. Labs are great swimmers. They have **webbing** between their toes. Webbing is extra skin. The webbing allows labs to use their paws like paddles to move easily through water. Labs also have oily coats that allow water to slide off, which helps keep labs warm in water.

Labs love to swim at beaches!

Slow starts

If your lab has never been in water, it may be scared to swim at first. Never force your lab into water. Take your lab to the beach and allow it to follow you into the water. Swim around and let your lab follow you. Before long, your pet will be the first one in water!

Safety rules

Your lab will probably love swimming, but you have to make sure that your lab is safe. Follow the rules below to keep your lab safe near water.

- Never let your lab swim in water that has strong **currents**. Currents are rushing waves that could pull your lab under the water.

- Never let your lab swim in unclean water.

Never let your lab swim by itself. Keep a close eye on your lab whenever it is in the water.

Do not let your lab swim for long periods of time. Your lab may not know when it is too tired to keep swimming.

If your lab is swimming in a pool, make sure it has a way to get out easily. Give your pet a bath after it swims in a pool.

Staying safe

Most labs are friendly, but you must still respect their **territory**, or personal space. Your lab may become angry if you try to take away food it is eating or a toy with which it is playing. Your pet may bite you to protect its space. You must train your lab to share its territory with you and the rest of your family.

Do not bother your lab while it is eating. When it is finished, your lab will be happy to play with you.

Be aware

Your lab may warn you that it is getting angry. If your lab is getting ready to attack, it may show its teeth and stare at you. If your lab behaves this way, do not look it in the eyes. Stand still and hold your arms at your sides. Say "good dog" in a soothing voice to try to calm down the dog. Do not run away or yell at your lab. When the dog calms down, tell an adult how the dog behaved.

Be gentle with your lab. If you treat your lab gently, it will be gentle with you.

Visiting a vet

As soon as you get your lab, take it to see a vet. The vet will check the lab to make sure it is healthy. When necessary, the vet will give your lab **vaccinations** with needles. The vaccinations will help protect your lab from becoming ill. Take your lab to the vet once a year for a checkup.

As labs get older, many develop hip problems that make it difficult for them to walk. Your vet will be able to treat your lab's hip problems.

No unwanted puppies!

You should have your lab **neutered**. A neutered dog cannot make puppies. If you let your lab have puppies, you will have to work hard to find good homes for all the puppies.

Warning signs

If your lab seems sick, take it to the vet immediately. Watch for the warning signs listed below.

- Take your lab to the vet right away if it is vomiting, fainting, or limping.

- Your lab may be sick if its eyes or ears are red or unclean.

If you feel any lumps on your lab's body, your dog may be ill.

A sick lab may drink more water than usual. It may also stop eating.

Your lab may be sick if it is losing clumps of fur, if it is sleeping more than usual, or if it is not playful.

With proper care and a lot of love, your lab will be a part of your family for many years!

Words to know

Note: Boldfaced words that are defined in the book may not appear on this page.

affect To have an influence or effect on something

animal shelter A place that cares for animals that do not have owners

avalanche A large amount of snow that falls suddenly down a mountainside

breeder A person who brings dogs together so the dogs can make puppies

consistent Describing behavior that does not change over time

dairy food Food made with milk and milk products

emergency A dangerous, unexpected situation

fisher A person who fishes

microchipped Describing an animal that has a small device placed under its skin

physically challenged Describes a person who has a physical condition that limits his or her movements

styptic powder A powder used to stop a dog's nails from bleeding

train To teach a dog how to behave

vaccination A way of protecting a body against diseases

veterinarian A doctor who treats animals

Index

1 2 3 4 5 6 7 8 9 0 Printed in the U.S.A. 5 4 3 2 1 0 9 8 7 6